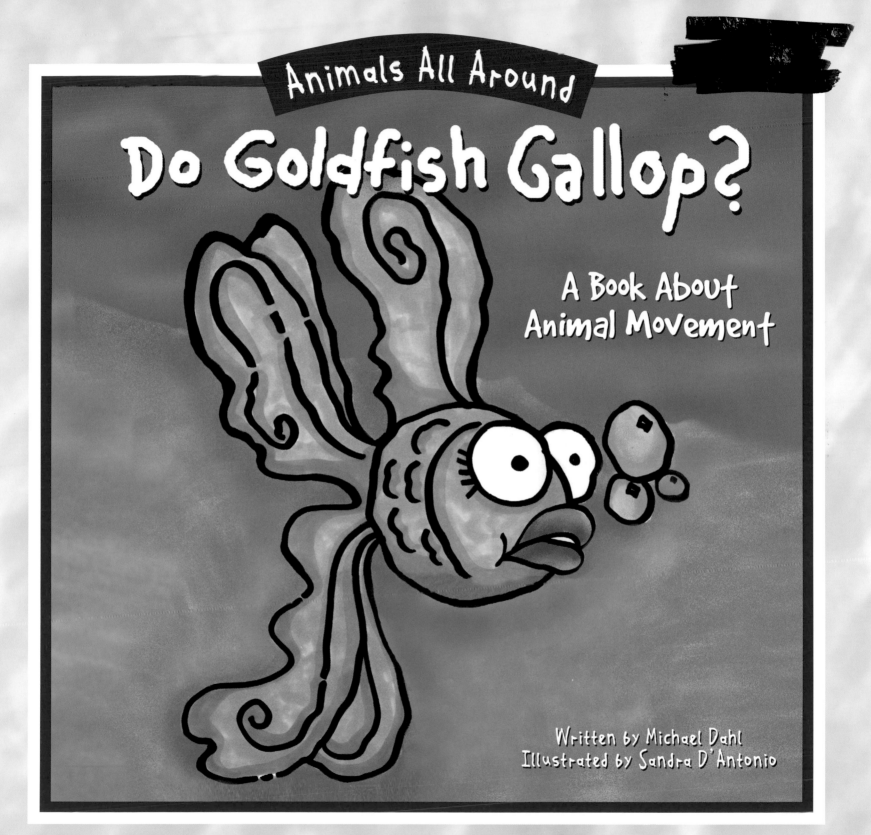

Animals All Around

Do Goldfish Gallop?

A Book About Animal Movement

Written by Michael Dahl
Illustrated by Sandra D'Antonio

Content Consultant: Kathleen E. Hunt, Ph.D.
Research Scientist and Lecturer, Zoology Department
University of Washington, Seattle, Washington

Reading Consultant: Susan Kesselring, M.A., Literacy Educator
Rosemount-Apple Valley-Eagan (Minnesota) School District

PICTURE WINDOW BOOKS
MINNEAPOLIS, MINNESOTA

Animals All Around series editor: Peggy Henrikson
Page production: The Design Lab
The illustrations in this book were rendered in marker.

Picture Window Books
5115 Excelsior Boulevard
Suite 232
Minneapolis, MN 55416
1-877-845-8392
www.picturewindowbooks.com

Printed in the United States of America.
1 2 3 4 5 6 08 07 06 05 04 03

Library of Congress Cataloging-in-Publication Data
Dahl, Michael.
Do goldfish gallop? / written by Michael Dahl ; illustrated by
Sandra D'Antonio.
p. cm. — (Animals all around)
Summary: Describes how different animals get from one place
to another.
ISBN 1-4048-0105-7 (lib. bdg.)
1. Animal locomotion—Juvenile literature. [1. Animal locomotion.]
I. D'Antonio, Sandra, 1956— ill. II. Title.
QP301 .D24 2003
591.47'9—dc21
2002155160

Do Goldfish Gallop?

No! Zebras gallop.

When zebras run as swiftly as they can, they gallop like horses. Most zebras live on open grasslands, with few places to hide. They have to run fast to get away from animals that might attack them.

4

Do goldfish hop?

No! Kangaroos hop.

Kangaroos use their huge hind legs to hop from place to place. They can hop much faster than people can run. Their long tails swing up and down to help them hop.

Do goldfish paddle?

No! Ducks paddle.

A duck has wide feet with flaps of skin, or webs, between the toes. Webbed feet work like flippers to help the duck paddle in the water.

Do goldfish pounce?

No! Panthers pounce.

When a panther attacks, it pounces on other animals from behind. Thick pads on the bottoms of the panther's paws help the cat move silently and surprise its prey. The panther's powerful legs spring into action for long leaps.

Do goldfish slither?

No! Snakes slither.

A snake slithers in a smooth and slinky wave as it glides over grass or twists around tree trunks. Strong muscles help its long, scaly body move smoothly over the ground.

Do goldfish climb?

No! Geckos climb.

Gecko lizards can climb straight up a slippery window.

They scoot up and down trees and walls and around smooth rocks.

Special pads on a gecko's toes help the lizard cling to any surface.

Do goldfish swing through trees?

No! Gibbons swing through trees.

Gibbons have long arms that are good for swinging from branch to branch. Tall trees are safe places for gibbons to sleep, eat, and play.

Do goldfish dig through dirt?

No! Earthworms dig through dirt.

Earthworms dig in the dark, damp dirt, pushing forward with open mouths. They swallow dirt and bits of dead plants as they move. Earthworms leave the dirt looser and richer.

Do goldfish jump through grass?

No! Grasshoppers jump through grass.

Grasshoppers have thick, powerful thighs.
Their legs bend backwards. These special legs
help grasshoppers jump through the tallest grass.
Grasshoppers can jump up to 20 times their own body length.

Do goldfish swim?

Yes! Goldfish swim.
Shimmering goldfish,
sleek and slim—
shimmering goldfish
swish and swim.

How and Where Animals Move

Animals move above our heads.

swing and sway	gibbons
climb and cling	geckos

Animals move below our feet.

slither and slink	snakes
dig and wiggle	earthworms

Animals move through the water.

paddle and splash	ducks
swish and swim	goldfish

Animals hop and jump and race.

pad and pounce	panthers
hop high	kangaroos
jump with a jerk	grasshoppers

Animals run with other animals.

gallop in a great group	zebras

Words to Know

gallop—to run so fast that all four legs leave the ground at once

pounce—to leap on something and grab it

prey—an animal that is hunted by another animal for food

slither—to slide along. Snakes have no legs, so they have to slither instead of walk.

thighs—the upper part of some animals' legs. A grasshopper's strong thighs help it jump far.

webbed feet—feet that have flaps of skin between the toes. Webbed feet help ducks paddle.

Index

To Learn More

At the Library

Brett, Jessica. *Animals on the Go*. San Diego: Harcourt, 2000.

Davis, Katie. *Who Hops?* San Diego: Red Wagon Books, 2002.

Hall, Peg. *Whose Feet Are These? A Look at Hooves, Paws, and Claws*. Minneapolis: Picture Window Books, 2003.

London, Jonathan. *Wiggle, Waggle*. San Diego: Harcourt Brace, 2002.

Walsh, Melanie. *Do Donkeys Dance?* Boston: Houghton Mifflin, 2000.

On the Web

Minnesota Zoo
http://www.mnzoo.com/index.asp
Explore the Minnesota Zoo online, including a Family Farm. See pictures of the animals and visit the Kids' Corner with animal puzzles, games, and coloring sheets.

Zoological Society of San Diego: e-zoo
http://www.sandiegozoo.org/virtualzoo/homepage.html
Visit this virtual zoo with a Kid Territory. The section for kids includes animal profiles, games, zoo crafts, and even animal-theme recipes, such as Warthog Waffles.

Want to learn more about how animals move?
Visit FACT HOUND at http://www.facthound.com.